SESAME STREET®

All about
GROCERY STORE WORKERS

Susan B. Katz

Lerner Publications ◆ Minneapolis

Who are the people in your neighborhood?

Sesame Street has always been set smack in the middle of a friendly, busy community. We know that for all children, getting to know their communities is crucially important. So is understanding that everyone in the neighborhood—including kids!—has a part to play. In the *Sesame Street® Loves Community Helpers* books, *Sesame Street*'s favorite furry friends help young readers get to know some of these helpers better.

Sincerely,
The Editors at
Sesame Workshop

Table of Contents

Grocery Store Workers Are Fantastic!

Me love grocery store workers. They help me find food. Mmmmm.

Why We Love Grocery Store Workers

Lots of people work in grocery stores. Grocery store workers are important community helpers.

I wave and say hi to the grocery store workers.

Grocery store workers bring carts to the front of the store. Shoppers grab a cart or a basket to bring around the store.

While we shop, my daddy and I put things we want to buy in our cart.

Grocery store workers put the fruits and vegetables in the same section of the store. Behind the deli counter, they slice meats and cheeses.

Bakers work in the bakery. They decorate birthday cakes and bake things like bread, bagels, and muffins.

In the aisles, grocery store workers put boxes and bags of food in their place. That's called stocking the shelves.

I am tall and can reach the top shelves!

Grocery store workers know where everything is kept. They can help shoppers find things.

Since grocery store workers are so helpful, there's no need for Super Grover today.

Some foods have to stay cold. Grocery store workers put foods like frozen vegetables and ice cream in the freezer aisles.

When we get home, I help my mommy put the frozen fruit in our freezer.

They put milk and eggs in the refrigerated section.

Grocery store workers can help me find butter so my abuela and I can make cookies.

I put everything on the counter.

After you finish shopping, it is time to check out.

The cashier is very friendly.

23

The cashier tells you how much to pay.
Some stores have baggers.
A bagger puts your groceries in a shopping bag.

I help count the money when my mom pays.

Then it's time to bring your groceries home! When you're finished shopping, you put the cart away and thank the grocery store workers for their help.

Grocery store workers always help shoppers have a great visit.

Thank You, Grocery Store Workers!

Dear Grocery Store Worker,

Thank you very much for your hard work. And for helping me find veggies me like! Me think your job is very important.

Your friend,

Cookie Monster

You take turn now! Write thank-you note to grocery store worker.

Picture Glossary

cashier: a person who scans the groceries, takes your money, and gives you change

community: a place where people live and work

deli counter: a place where people can go to pick out meats and cheeses to be sliced and wrapped

stocking: putting food in its place

Read More

Murray, Julie. *Grocery Store Workers*. Minneapolis: Abdo Kids Junior, 2021.

Press, J. P. *Grocery Stores*. Minneapolis: Bearport, 2021.

Walker, Alan. *When I Go to the Grocery Store*. New York: Crabtree, 2021.

Index

Photo Acknowledgments

Image credits: Fuse/Getty Images, p. 5; Drazen_/Getty Images, pp. 6, 30 (top right); Jon Feingersh Photography Inc/Getty Images, p. 7; Images By Tang Ming Tung/Getty Images, p. 8; Tetra Images/ Getty Images, p. 9; xavierarnau/Getty Images, pp. 10, 30 (bottom left); BearFotos/Shutterstock. com, p. 11; LightFieldStudios/Getty Images, p. 12; Zero Creatives/Getty Images, p. 13; jacoblund/Getty Images, p. 14 (bottom right); Jacobs Stock Photography/Getty Images, pp. 15, 19, 23, 30 (top left); Aleksandar Malivuk/Shutterstock.com, p. 16; Keith Brofsky/Getty Images, p. 17; SDI Productions/ Getty Images, p. 18; Prostock-studio/Shutterstock.com, p. 20; wavebreakmedia/Shutterstock. com, p. 21; Ariel Skelley/Getty Images, p. 22; Pressmaster/Shutterstock.com, p. 24; Edwin Tan/ Getty Images, p. 25; Hispanolistic/Getty Images, p. 26; eclipse_images/Getty Images, p. 27; Monkey Business Images/Shutterstock.com, p. 29.

Cover image: Jon Feingersh Photography Inc/Getty Images.

Lerner Publications Company
An imprint of Lerner Publishing Group, Inc.
241 First Avenue North
Minneapolis, MN 55401 USA

For reading levels and more information, look up this title at www.lernerbooks.com.

Main body text set in Mikado Medium.
Typeface provided by HVD Fonts.

Editor: Brianna Kaiser **Designer:** Mary Ross

Library of Congress Cataloging-in-Publication Data

Names: Katz, Susan B., 1971- author.
Title: All about grocery store workers / Susan B. Katz.
Description: Minneapolis : Lerner Publications, 2023. | Series: Sesame Street loves community
    helpers | Includes bibliographical references and index. | Audience: Ages 4–8 | Audience: Grades
    K–1 | Summary: "Come along with favorite Sesame Street characters in celebrating grocery store
    workers. From helping guests find what they need to shelving merchandise, grocery store workers
    are important community helpers"– Provided by publisher.
Identifiers: LCCN 2021036062 | ISBN 9781728456157 (library binding) | ISBN 9781728463827
    (paperback) | ISBN 9781728462127 (ebook)
Subjects: LCSH: Grocery trade—Employees—Juvenile literature.
Classification: LCC HD9320.5 .K37 2022 | DDC 381/.456413—dc23

LC record available at https://lccn.loc.gov/2021036062

Manufactured in the United States of America
1-50685-50104-2/9/2022